# Aching to be Human

# Aching to be Human

Stormy Abel

atmosphere press

# Table of Contents

There is no feeling, no hope, no suffering that can't be explained
by the words of a poet. It may not be of my own eloquent
sequence. But out there in the masses of literature new or
ancient: there has been some prolific expansion of the beating
that your heart feels. And it's beautiful, almost biblical.
Religion is a scapegoat. But these humans that have tread the
great emotional waters of the world who were brave enough
to tell the stories of the heart- are something to believe in.

# Writing Abandonment

There are a million different broken homes. Each with their
  cracks in unique places.

There is a big difference from abandon and broken. Broken is the
  home still lived in-abandoned is the ache of the emptiness.

Too many to fathom are the people left with the wreckage. Ghost
  stuck in the frame of what once went by "home" is now house.

The home I know is not a home at all. It's a multitude of abandon
  places that I have recollections of being alone.

Alone in the chaos, alone in the silence. Alone in the shifted
  foundation, cracked walls and caving roofs.

With paint peeling and my heart bleeding I lived. I breathed the
  dust until it sunk into my lungs.

My abandon home became my abandoned heart.

# Robbed from the Start

Somebody robbed me
Somebody took me away from me before I even got a chance to
    know myself
I didn't even get the most important pieces,
I can't even search within myself because I am road blocked, body
    shocked
They took me for no good reason.
They took with such ease of hand.
Do they even know what they have
Do they know they left me with nothing
Not even myself.
Somebody created a shell of a person wishing to know what it's
    like to be real.
Somebody created an empty heart that never got a chance to be
    pure
They created a heart that can't love
They created a heart with chambers that don't work properly
Vessels pump air into my body
I'm left with ache for the blood to be in my veins
An ache to be human.

Charity

You passed your sickness down to me.
You should have never procreated.
The illness inside you runs through my veins, too.
I want to hate you, and I want to erase you.
Mother is not a name you go by and love is not a feeling I reserve
    for you.
Charity.
What a name for such a selfish person.
In some twisted way, I understand you.
It doesn't make anything excusable, but I get you.
You're lost and alone in your own head.
Thoughts you don't want to possess destroy you.
You feel diminished and in most ways you are.
You're a vessel of skin around rotted flesh.
A beating heart that's off track and a mind you can't control.
A glimmer of you wanted to be better, but you let the ill of
    darkness consume you.
You bathe in it, lather up.
You play in it even when the sun comes up.
I know because it's in me too.
I'm stronger than you, "mom."
I see what you let yourself become.
That won't be me.
So, I'll keep fighting.

# Hoping for More Than Hope

Does writing like this even help?
Can it free my mind of floors full of shattered glass I trip over with
    every thought?
I don't know what it does or what it helps but I need something.
Desperate for anything that makes a small space of clarity in here.
It's getting hard to breath.
The air is filled with sand and my lungs are getting heavy.
Life's always been hard; is it always going to be hard?
Is it set in stone?
Find a ladder upwards and it starts to creek with every higher
    step.
You feel like you are getting off the ground a little bit, and it
    breaks.
You hold on, and you get splinter filled hands.
Hope won't keep you up there.
Hope won't hold you steady.
You're going to get knocked down.
Holding on will only make it worse.
Let go and start again.
Climb a new ladder only to fall again.
That's the summary of what this life is so far.
Hopefully I'm wrong.
Hopefully I'll get through the glass.
Hopefully I'll find something better than hope.

# Bee

To the furiously brave bee that nurtures life
And the one who destroyed everything in efforts of saving herself
All while stinging someone else, leaving half of her in them
For without her madness I would not believe in life like I do
I wouldn't believe in myself at all
And these words surely wouldn't exist

## Moon Sleeper

I guess you've been sleeping with the moon
Looks like possibility waiting on a blank page
The crescent holds you better
The starting of a new cycle
Gives you more hope in the discomfort
The full sky and stars at your bedside
Light up your heart in the dark night
Conversations with the sun don't bleed right
Humming the melancholy melody of the moon
Lullaby for your demons in sight
Maybe if something can lure them to rest
When the sun comes up
You won't be out of breath

# Cosmic Collison

The language we first spoke was not of our own mouth
Some ancient ways of the same lost sea
Words of not sound or motion
More waves of the universe
In just the right frequency
To collide in delicate harmony
We spoke a language that created a wormhole in reality

Both of lost things, unknown and forgotten
Found more than what anyone could go looking for
We pulled love from behind the stars
Fought gravity to keep it on earth

# Unwavering


You looked at me with eyes of a silent
promise
Spine creeping out the curve of your back
Begging to be touched
With all the harshness and softness of you
unsaid
unspoken

# Heart Rhythm

The way you tap the beats out on my wrist
The pulse I never knew I needed
Just the right amount of life
And sadness
The way the sunlight finds rest on your skin
The pallet of my daydreams
Just the right amount of ease

# Dive Deep

The air doesn't feel heavy but your breath does
My heart drums on my ribcage like an awakening
Your fingertips soft and sweet
Blood runs hot, brings boiling life to my body
Ignite me gently, slowly but with a fire all the same
Your secret pull and ache to explore more
Your eyes draw on my skin, but your lips fulfill the pattern we're
    in
Pause an inch away
And it only makes me want to dive in

# Caged Heart

I have trouble showing what resides in my heart. It's a cage; I
constantly fight to get out of. It hurts that I can't show what I
feel, when it's right on the brink behind locked bars. Small
pieces get through the metal gaps, but not all of it. Not the
intensity that I feel within myself. Not what I desperately want
to share with you.

Your feelings do matter immensely to me. I feel you inside the
rattle of my bones. I feel what you say and do. The good and
the bad. I feel it so much so that it's overwhelming. It's difficult
to live with so much inside and so little outwardly showing.
It's a trap that I'm caught in. I want to show and act upon how
I feel. The more I try to pull it up my throat, the quicker my air
ways collapse.

Maybe the hurt finds a way out. Maybe the hurt explodes out of
my being like a time bomb. I throw up my guts to the ground
and my mouth spits out punches like gathered saliva on the
back of my tongue. It spews out to anyone in radial distance.
The hurt finds a target and escapes.

I'm sorry.

I'm sorry for wounds created by the bomb and for the shrapnel
that gets wedged in your heart. As my chest cavity breaks by
the force of the bomb, I feel it breaking you, too. In haste of
the panic from the bitter taste of metal and hurt in my mouth,
I continue. Because something got out of the cage. Something
inside broke free. Something is coming out, so I let it come. I
let it take you down.

It's not my intention.

I don't ask you to tend to my feelings. I don't ask you to do more
than you wish to. I know it's not fair to love a heart that pumps
air.

I have given you more than anyone. My arms dangle out of the
cage to touch you. And sometimes I think they do. I'm locked
away. I'm confined even away from myself. I give you more of
me than I can even give myself. You desire more of me, and
the truth is... I have held that same desire for years.

I have lived within a broken body and a caged heart. It sounds like
bullshit, but you've been mending it. I have seen parts of
myself that I didn't even know were alive. You have been
creating life inside of this body bag.

# Love Between Her Shoulder Blades

The softness of your skin, that small indent that my thumb lays
    perfectly in
I nuzzle my face against your back
Between your shoulder blades
I silently breathe you in
You fill my lungs and expand my heart, oh god I don't want to
    drift apart
I want to hold on to this small maybe last moment of moments
    had with you
My life has never made more sense than in your hands
Don't leave
I'm not okay, I don't want to face the day
How do I walk away
Please don't let your love for me fade
It was for you which my soul was made

Un Grip

Challenge and change go hand in hand
As they always have
My challenge is you and my change is me
So I'll take you by the hand
I'll let my fingers wrap around yours with ease
It's the letting go that I can't un grip
As it always is

# Buffet

You're forgetting what makes us unique
It's like you've adapted a blindness
Short sighted
Of what shaped our soul
I am ready to jump out of my skin
Waiting for you
I lay myself out as a buffet for you
And you pass up supper like you got drunk at brunch
I want you
Your churning stomach aches for something
Of substance
Run your fingers down my spine
Anything but gently

Stop

I don't know if love is leaving you
I don't know if the parts of me inside of you are dying out
I don't know anything

If you're moving on, please ... love me enough to tell me that. Love
    me enough to tell me to stop waiting for you. If your
    intentions aren't the same as mine, tell me. Because I promise;
    I am too strong willed to quit, if you don't tell me to. I will
    always believe there is a way.

## Summer Flu

Caress and cradle
These old wounds cracking open
Seeping out like cold sweat
From a hot summer flu
Drenched and aching
I can't tell if I'm sleeping
Or waking

Maybe I'm baking
In these long-lost sorrows
I didn't think they would
Interrupt my tomorrows

Hold me in this
Familiar sickness

# Suffocated at Some Point

I think at some point this relationship stopped feeling like a
     choice that you believed in.
You stopped breathing me in, rejected the scent of my skin.
You became suffocated by me breathing your air, acted like it was
     a sin.
You slowly started storing oxygen, just for you.
You left me gasping, a cyanotic shade of blue.
You even neglected to mention my change of hue.
Your love asphyxiated me; you didn't even have to use your
     hands.
I think at some point I stopped feeling like home to you.

# Panic Attack

Picking old wounds
Pry them open to ooze sorrowed blood
Again
Just to taste the iron in my mouth
Walking around with lungs filled with
Sand
This heavy chest is familiar
Faint breathing with no filter
Panic attack
Eyes glazed over from the haunting
Staying awake is daunting
Blurred vision

# Running

I'm a refugee
Seeking safety in a warm body
in anything other than me

I'm a displaced person, with a deserter soul
Running away from everything
away from myself

I'm an estranged stray, with no home and no place
Roaming to find anything that will look twice
anything that will carry me far from my heart

I'm a down-and-out vagrant
Down to nothing
to the last piece of me

# Crooked

You'd never know you were inside the body of a ghost
A hologram with an undetectable image that even you can't see
    past
A mirror that's looking at a mirror will never know the true image
A crooked halo above your head
A load of men in your bed
You'd never know you were inside the belly of the beast
A endless pit of sorrow and decay, ripe smell, cheap hell
A cocktail that God himself couldn't undo
A thrill for moment
A pattern that beats with a crooked heart

## Graveyard

Retreat to within
Put my vocabulary in coffins
Buried in my bruised bones
Constant visits to the tomb stone
Of what use to flow freely
Eyes filled form mirrors within
I can't see out of my past
6ft down
The outside world is a blur to me
In this graveyard I carry

VM

I've listened to your voicemail 3 times a day
For weeks
It doesn't mean I can talk to you
You are the pavement beneath my tires
These white lines I've painted on you
Are ones I cannot cross

# Untitled Torment

Can't put a title on the words
Can't keep running from meaning
Numbing my mind
Has left me aching
For blood on the pages
I'm dripping dusty
Driving drunk
Lost my license
Can't keep empty writing
Can't put aside the desolation

# Silent Mask

Life is not always a gift
Sometimes it's a hopeless curse
To the girl I once knew
I still see you in the mirror
I can't find who is hiding in your skin
If you knew you would become a shell
Would you leave in the same silence as before
Are you okay with this echoing excuse
For a woman who wears your mask

# Heroin

Venom by your bedside
Black rain falling from your sky
The trees shed in the dark daylight
Shaky hands down the drain
Mind melting from the sight
Great heights
Many nights
Love you right
In your fight
I won't let you decay
Break the urge to stay
Lock the gates, turn away

Blackness
Won't take you
This day

# APT #62

It was light-hearted, high-pitched laughter
It was a heavy, misguided, silent slaughter
We kept our love like rancid leftovers
Sitting in the refrigerator until it was molded
Maybe this love wasn't forever
We kept it past the expiration date
Remembering how good it once tasted
We let everything go but each other
It was staying in bed, all day, intertwined
It was getting high and out of mind
It was a filthy house
Everything strung out
It was dishes in the sink
It was past due rent
It was driving to escape

The home we made

# No Place for Shame

I had a dream I held your face
Cried in your wake
Your skin smelled the same
Here in my hands there is no place for shame
Your brown eyes peered into me softly
Dark to cover up the suffering seeping inside
I only ever wanted to hold you right
You reached for me
Like you'd been lacking me
My bones shake and shatter
I thought I didn't matter
Love doesn't leave
I think it just finds a new place to breathe
Touch me
I am here

# Prayer

I've always said that writing was a mirror
Maybe it's more of a prayer
I've never prayed until I found myself pleading
With the pages until my fingers bled
My words ran dry
Upon an unanswered petition to the ink
Crucified myself for sake of her
Inhaled our memories like Holy Communion
To remember that love did exist
I bare the cross of her when I wake
Carry her around like a lost religion
Only I believe in
Praying to a blank page
Subsisting in the conviction
For something no longer living

# Monster

Bad love hears me coming back
It's patiently waiting for the return of my hallowing steps
Aching to make a meal of everything I lack

Easily taste the fright in the sweat on my skin
It's pouring me down the throat of a beast untamed
Feeding its appetite with this toxic battle of sin

Identifying the unforgiving shadows that haunt
Preying on the weaknesses that taunt

Can't help but mercilessly draw me in
You lie awake in the casket I mourn you in

## 5,4,3,2,1

Lately I find you with my eyes closed
5 months
I know nothing of your life
Lately I've been drinking to go to sleep
4 months
Black out nights
Lately you've been vacant
3 months
Poison in your bloodstream
Lately we've been different people
2 months
Searching for me
Lately time dances in slow motion
1 month
Hoping to find you

*Hazy Living*

I miss how it felt
To step outside and not be afraid
To feel alive
I long for the days
That the sun sometimes hurt
It doesn't phase me in the haze
You're like a fogy morning in my mind
But you last for days, weeks, months
...it's been a year

And I miss me

# Happy Valentine's Day

I'm leaving with my underwear in my pocket
She says I've been crying in my sleep again
I keep you in this unforgiving locket
I don't know where I've been
Lacking better synonyms

She doesn't know you're in this bed too
She doesn't know your name is written on the tears left on her
    pillow
She doesn't know that you haunt the sweat in her sheets

I feel nothing but you and she bides the time
Fuck a rhyme

In the mist of all that awakens life in the morning
You were my downpour
At first it quenched my thirst
Until you made a monsoon of me
Drowned me into the nightfall
Wouldn't answer my 2am call

# Twenty-Two

22 weird blue
I've got used to living in this hue
It's four in the morning
My head is swarming
The sun is going to take over the stars
I guess it's time to go to bed with these scars
I'll sow and patch my leaky heart
Maybe tomorrow will be a new start

## Illusive Elements

change happens on a strange unmeasurable scale
teetering on the seesaw, forward and backward
it mirrors life's balance on the edge of all emotion

time is only perception
overlapping and gasping for more
yet always giving less

hope comes and I can't let it go
clings to me with the stench of you
it remains in place of famine in the heart

love lingers unforgivingly, like a stain or tattoo
nobody can see what it leaves on you
cruel with the way its ink seeps too deep

you are a beautiful disaster hanging on by a thread
self-sabotage your passions and dreams away
buried underneath the pain

echoing through my bones

# Noose

Closets are for the darkness
And I can't unclench my grip
There's a noose behind the door
It's been there for a year
Patient threads holding an unnamed comfort
For weeks it dangled in the spotlight
On the front side
Teasing of a place better than here
Knot made just the right size
The promise of a defeated heartbeat

## Maternal Disquietude

I go through the same stages as you
The ones where we silently lose
Living on a bruise
When we wear our hair up
In the middle spot
A little low
Un-brushed
Months of being
Untouched

# Have You Healed?

I haven't seen what you look like in a while
Have you changed
Are you hallow
I haven't heard your voice in months
Is it the same
Does it echo
I haven't occupied your touch in a year
Do you still feel
Are you real

## Finding Paper

I think I've been terrified of the words that haven't hit the page yet
I've been writing short, softly
I think I've been writing to everything that is not me
I don't know if I can handle reliving myself, seeing me again
The last time took me out of my body, put my soul in front of me
I'm not sure if I liked the tragedy before my eyes
Those words were mine?

I've been writing so that I can put you in my life again
Even if it's only in ink
I've been writing so that I can hold you like I use to
Love you better in the things I never said

# Get Well Soon

Embody the moment you're in
Instead of being a shell of your past
Walking around in hallow skin
And brittle bones
Plagued of memory

# D.R.A.F.T.


I'll call this a rough draft of myself before I know who I am.
I'll let this be messy: permanent ink.
I'll take it with the misspellings, scratch outs and words forgotten.
Permission to be ugly in the truth of words unspoken.
I haven't written elegantly for months.
It all taste like you and sometimes it makes me sick.
I used to think writing this was brave, maybe I baited it on an
    imaginary hook you'd never see.
I'm fishing in empty waters and not publishing my book.

## Anchor

I need to find an anchor to myself
My own depths are carrying me away
Touch the fire
Just to feel
Set one
Just to heal

# Stitching Yourself

Maybe the black hole is your heart. It eats at you until you've been
　　devoured before your own eyes. It makes a feast of you.
For dessert, it reminds you of all your lost parts in the darkness.

You over anticipate the weight your heart can bare.
You take it anyway.
You sew the stitches in your heart so tightly so you can burry
　　things inside, so you can carry, so you can hold.
But it fails.
When the stitches start to unravel things deep inside slowly seep
　　out like poison, it hits you again and again.
You stitch yourself back up and try to gather the escaped pieces,
　　poking them back in the hole that they just fell from.
Your heart weighs down your ribcage and becomes a strain for
　　you to breath.
But you take another breath.
You overload your heart and hold it desperately in place because
　　you have no other choice.
Maybe you don't.
You clench your fist at a world that has done you wrong and beat
　　you down. You hold your white knuckled grip ready to punch
　　back at it.
But it's too much.
Too much has pushed you down, too much has infiltrated your
　　mind, and too much has been a parasite in you.

You keep going. You fight for each breath that leads to another
　　heart beat, even if you don't want to admit it.
You breathe and that is so beautiful.
You fill your heavy soul with new oxygen again and again.
You slowly revive yourself.
You live.
Your heavy heart beats.
You preserve.
You draw new strength.

You stitch yourself and go forward.
You feel.
You see.
You are more human than anyone.
You are more alive than anyone.
You have a better chance than anyone to make it through this life.

This fight in you, this eternal war, is what makes you human.

## Twisted Tongue


Break into the ribcage holding this heart of swarming ghosts
Let them be free so that I can breathe
Make them stop crawling up the throat of a tongue that's tired of
     forgiving
So that I can swallow, love again
Shatter the bones made of all my demons
For I am done with them

# Dreams Pushed Aside

I may bend and brake
But I am no ones to take
In the days I've spent too long
Trying to untangle the strings
Of my heart
I forgot to live at the start
Where these dreams
Didn't just sit on my back
They were the iris of my eyes
Now I look behind
At all the time spent
Holding myself together
For nothing more than
Not knowing any better
Scraping by on life
Trying to make some sort of
Shelter

# Breathing Tomorrows

You cannot exist in the same prosaic routine
Breathing air from one day into the next
It's not enough substance to feed your soul
Heart beating for tomorrow
Shuts off the life of today
You cannot keep running
Into the ground
What we thought
We had found

It's not enough

# Harvest

Springtime harvest
Of all the flowers
That bloomed
Resilient
Despite winter
Sorrows

# Sleep Well

Find some peace in the still air
Let today be at rest
Let tomorrow be what it will
And find yourself
In the middle
Hold on to the woman inside
That is stronger than the
Woman of mere daylight hours
You are not confined
In this painted prism
Let the nighttime sea
Behind the clouds
Fill your heart
Of no false stars

Dream sweet.

In the Middle

I'm somewhere between a torturous ache
And a marvelous break
Both something I feel ill equipped for
The haunting must come to an end
I'm stuffed full of things I cannot mend

I won't let my heart take any more blows
At the hand of someone that makes me feel less
Than me
Like my peace is lacking
Because you're not in it
Like you used to be

# Yellow Belly

I am not a home for the faint of heart
I am not a place for cowards' refuge
Because I won't let you run from yourself
There is no escaping in the night
I hold you to who you are
Call it forsaken sight
Drown in the daylight
If you come with a mouth full of yellow-belly promises
You can leave with your gutless fever
There is no place for me either

# Whale

Maybe to find more of yourself
You must dip into the survival of your past
The yesterdays that swallowed you whole
The whale of life that spit you out unforgivingly
Go back to the belly of the beast
Go back to your darkest days
Your truest self lies in your truest suffering aches
In some profound ways you found yourself
Lost yourself too
Find the parts of yourself that you let go
The existence of you that led to remain and regain
In an art form that can't be explained
You are not whole, you left pieces along the way
Your fight today needs the strength of your yesterdays

# Snowflake Eyelashes

I've always lived in a writers head space. Wanting all of the
  experiences of my soul to live on through delicately shaped
  words; crafted from a type of magic magnitude I can't explain.
I wanted to hold the flowers that grew from my palms.
My desert spine with cactus bones and tumbleweed heart.
The bitterness of the darkness that held everything in its path in a
  forsaken limbo.
The bees that swarm my head with honey pouring out of my ears,
  all the sweetness escaping.
These nails brittle but fingers strong, white knuckle grip.
Hot breeze combating my snowflake eyelashes.
I see the world through a colored atmospheric trick that mocks
  reality.
Sometimes it's better than it was, and my chest beats fast,
  collapsing in these four walls.
Bound by no structure the ocean is freedom unknown.
I have broken every leaf and petal from my stem, cut my cement
  feet of broken seashells.
I have traveled here in all versions of my beaten skin and created
  a body of mixed stained glass.
Every glimmer from different shards of my past. Together
  reflecting nature- life- love.
And the light illuminating the glass?
Stormy; in the soft spring drizzle and the hurricane.
God's promise of a rainbow is false, but mine isn't.

Be unapologetic in your recovery. The process is not always
linear- it almost never is. It's okay if your healing is chaotic, if
you sometimes seek refuge where you shouldn't. It is alright if
you sometimes break your own heart too. It's okay because
the real process of mending the unthinkable is messy.
Unpredictable.


That is the beauty of being human.

Stormy Abel is a 23-year-old creative writer, author and artist. Being displaced at a young age left her torn with physical and emotional scarring. With a great deal of courage, she turned to writing as a way of honing the voice she had been silencing since childhood. While her writing career started as a deeply personal journey, she chose to publish her work because she found enlightenment and quiet solace in the honesty of poetry and prose. Abel shares her heart with raw candor. There is an intimacy about her writings, an unapologetic presentation of truths that might otherwise have a stigma about them. She writes on topics of mental illness, abuse, addiction, suicide and many other challenges. Her ambition is for readers to realize they possess strength in their sensitivity, tenderness in their vulnerability, and a glimmer in their darkest suffering. Ultimately that the darkness they carry, and the path to healing from it can be a beautiful part of the human condition.